SING SOLO SOPRANO

General Editor: John Carol Case

Edited by Jean Allister

First published by Oxford University Press 1985
Revised edition published 1986

These four volumes are presented with the needs of the younger singer in mind. Each book contains two operatic arias, two oratorio arias, two Lieder or songs in a foreign language, and English songs: a general collection covering a wide variety of periods, but specifically useful to the singer who wishes to gain valuable performing experience at a competitive festival, as a number of classes can be entered with all the necessary music contained in one volume.

Wherever possible Urtext editions, first editions or manuscripts have been consulted, and apart from breath marks which are always editorial, all other editorial markings are either shown in square brackets or as crossed slurs; these are offered as no more than a guide to performance in addition to the composer's own directions. Where further explanation is felt necessary, editorial suggestions are given in a footnote. All German, French and Italian songs are given in their original language together with a singing English translation or paraphrase. In most cases new translations have been specially made. New, simple and stylish piano realisations have been created for all the 'early' songs originally written with continuo accompaniment, and existing piano reductions of songs with orchestral accompaniment have been improved.

I would like to acknowledge the help I have received particularly from Julian Elloway of Oxford University Press, without whose help and guidance these volumes may well have foundered, and from Fiona Floate, his secretary, who coped with much arduous work in the background. I would also like to thank Richard Abram, René Atkinson, Clifford Bartlett, and Paul Keene, who have provided original texts and in some cases piano accompaniments. But above all, I would like to thank my editorial colleagues Jean Allister, Constance Shacklock, and Robert Tear, with whom, as always, it has been a pleasure to work.

John Carol Case

1. GAVOTTE
(1919)

Sir Henry Newbolt
(1862–1938)

HERBERT HOWELLS
(1892–1983)

Tempo di Gavotte [♩ = 104]

pp
4
p
Mem - ories long in mu - sic sleep - ing, No more sleep - ing, No more
tr
8
dumb;
pp
tr

Printed in Great Britain

OXFORD UNIVERSITY PRESS, MUSIC DEPARTMENT, GREAT CLARENDON STREET, OXFORD OX2 6DP

12
Del - i - cate phan - toms, soft - ly creep - ing Soft - ly
15
(poco rit. - - a tempo)
back from the old world come.
colla parte
19
Faint - est o - dours a-round them
22
stray - ing Sud-den-ly stray - ing In cham - bers dim, Whis - pering

25
silks in or - der sway - ing, Glim - mering gems on shoul - ders
28
mf
slim, Cour - age ad - vanc - ing, strong and ten - der, Grace un -
31
3
- ten - der Fan - ning de - sire; Sup - pliant con - quest, proud sur -
mf
34
cresc.
- ren - der, Cour - te - sy cold of hearts on fire, Wil - low - y,
mp
3
cresc.
p

poco allarg
bil - low - y, now they're bend - ing, Low they're bend-ing Down-dropt eyes; State - ly
poco
meas - ures and state - ly end - ings, Mu - sic sob - - - bing
colla voce
dim.
rit.
a tempo
and a dream that dies.
colla voce
Mem - ories long in mu - sic

53
sleep-ing, No more sleep-ing, No more dumb;
tr
8
Ped.
57
Del-i-cate phan-toms soft-ly
sempre pp
61
poco rit.
a tempo
creep-ing, Soft-ly back from the old world come.
ppp
64
tr
rit.

2. BY THY BANKS, GENTLE STOUR

WILLIAM BOYCE
(1711–79)
Piano accompaniment
by Elizabeth Poston

14
Voice with what trans - ports I swell'd the slow strain, Or re-
mf
R.H.
18
-turn'd dy - ing mea - sures In Ech - oes a - gain! Lit - tle
dolce
p colla voce
22
cu - pid beat Time, And the Gra - ces a - round Taught with
26
e - ven di - vis - ions To va - ry the sound, Taught with
più f

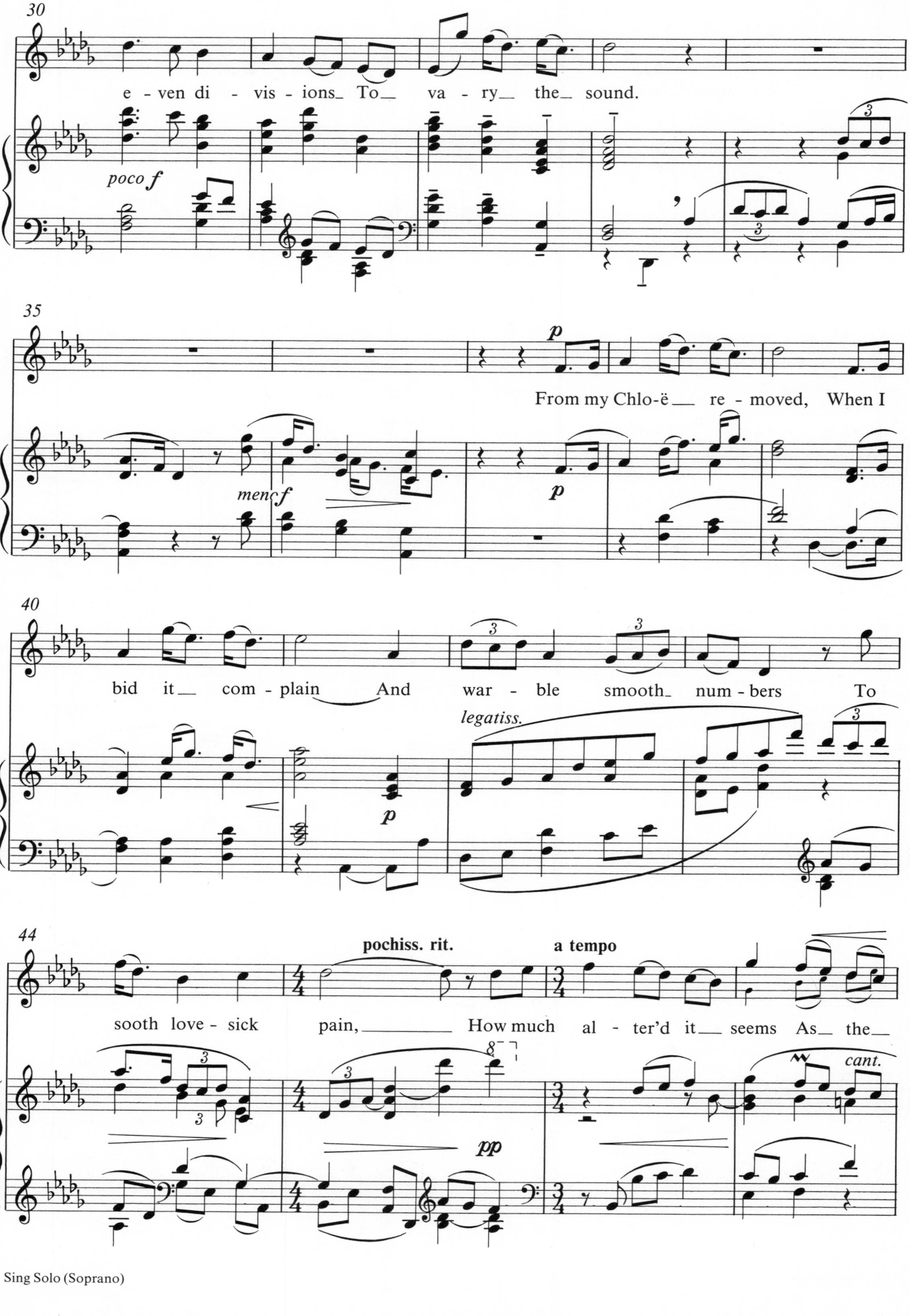
30
e - ven di - vis - ions_ To_ va - ry_ the_ sound.
poco f
35
p
From my Chlo-ë __ re - moved, When I
menof
p
40
bid it__ com - plain And war - ble smooth_ num - bers To
legatiss.
p
44
pochiss. rit.
a tempo
sooth love - sick pain,______ How much al - ter'd it__ seems As_ the__
pp
cant.

48
pochiss. rit. a piacere
ris - ing notes flow! And the soft fall - ing Strains How in - si - pid - ly
(Ossia) (Ossia)
colla voce
53
a tempo
più f
poco f
slow! I will play them no more, For 'tis her voice a - lone Must en-
58
poco allarg.
- rap - ture my Soul To en - li - ven its tone, Must en - rap - ture my
63
Soul To en - li - ven its tone!
f
8va

3. EN PRIÈRE

AT PRAYER

(1890)

Stéphan Bordèse
*Translation by Jean Allister

GABRIEL FAURÉ
(1845–1924)

Original key: E♭ major
*This translation has been revised for this new edition.

12
lois Sur la ter - re, Je sau - rai Vous ser -
earth, O my Fa - ther, I'll en - dea - vour to
sempre legato
cresc.
15
f
- vir, au - gus - te Roi des rois, Ô Lu - miè - re!
serve, O great-est King of Kings, Serve you ev - er;
f
18
p
Sur mes lè - vres, Sei - gneur, met - tez la vé - ri - té Sa - lu -
With my lips dear-est Lord, pro-claim the truth to all Who im -
p
21
mf
- tai - re, Pour que ce - lui qui doute, a - vec hu - mi - li -
- plore you, So that the souls who doubt, with great hu - mi - li -
mf

24
-té Vous ré-vè - re!
-ty May a-dore you.
p
Ne m'a-ban-don-nez
O leave me not a-
27
pas, donnez-moi la dou-ceur Né-ces-sai - re,
-lone, give me kind - ness and love, That with glad - ness
30
Pour a-pai-ser les maux, sou-la-ger la dou-leur, La mi-
I may re-dress all wrong, may con-sole all the grief, All the
33
-sè - - - re! Ré - vé-lez Vous à
sad - - - ness. O Fa-ther show the
sempre dolce

36
moi, Sei - gneur en qui je crois Et j'es -
way, and ev - er let me stay In your
39
- pè - - - re: Pour Vous je veux souf -
car - - - ing. For you I'll suf - fer
42
poco rit.
- frir et mou - rir sur la croix, Au Cal - vai - -
death, e - ven death on the cross, There at Cal - va -
46
a tempo
- re!
- ry.

4. DAS VEILCHEN

THE VIOLET

Kv476 (1785)

Johann Wolfgang Goethe
(1749–1832)
*Translation by Jean Allister

WOLFGANG AMADEUS MOZART
(1756–1791)

[Moderato ♩ = 69]
p
f
6
p
Ein Veil - chen auf der Wie - se stand, ge -
A vio - let in a mea - dow green had
10
- bückt in sich und un - be-kannt; es war ein her - zigs Veil - chen. Da
droop'd its head and grew un-seen: it was a charm - ing vi - o - let. There
f
p

The unbracketed dynamics are Mozart's; in the context of the song, *f* and *ff* may be interpreted more gently.

*This translation has been revised in bars 49 and 50 for this new edition.

15
kam ein' jun - ge Schä - fer - in mit leich - tem Schritt und mun - term Sinn da -
came a lit - tle shep - herd-ess with step so light, with face so bright; she
[mf]
19
- her, da - her, die Wie - se_ her und_ sang.
wan - dered thro' the mea - dow_ green and_ sang.
[p]
24
"Ach!" denkt das
"Ah!" thought the
28
Veil - chen,___ "wär' ich_ nur die schön-ste Blu-me der Na - tur, ach nur___
vi - o - let,___ "would that_ I had beau - ty rare be-yond com - pare per - haps___
[cresc.]

33
— ein_ klei - nes Weil-chen, bis mich das Lieb - chen ab - ge-pflückt und
— for_ one brief mo-ment; then let the dear one ga - ther me and
37
an dem Bu - sen matt - ge-drückt, ach_ nur, ach_ nur ein
press me to her ten - der-ly ah_ yes, ah_ yes for
41
[poco rall.]
[a tempo]
Vier - tel-stünd-chen lang!" Ach! A - ber ach! das Mäd-chen
one brief mo-ment sweet." Ah, but a - las! the maid-en
sf
p
46
kam und nicht in acht das Veil-chen nahm, er - trat
came and see - ing not the vio - let there she crushed
f

50
[p]
[rall.]
das ar - me Veil - chen. Es sank und starb und
the ten - der flow - er. It with - ered and died but
p
54
[a tempo]
[strin - gen - do]
freut' sich noch: "und sterb' ich denn, so sterb' ich doch durch
still rejoiced: "Though death may come, yet death will come through
cre - scen - do
57
[poco rall.]
sie! durch sie! zu ih-ren Fü - ßen doch!"
her, through her my own be - lo - ved."
f
61
a piacere
[p]
a tempo
Das ar - me Veil-chen! es war ein her - zigs Veil - chen.
Poor lit - tle vio - let! It was a charm - ing vi - o - let.
[p]
f
p

5. THE LOOM

Words by the arranger

Welsh Folk-song
Arr. GRACE WILLIAMS
(1906–1977)

13
mp
flown a - way, Flown a - way and left me all too soon, all too
p
17
p rall.
mp
soon, And, a - las, up - on my spir - it care was strewn, care was
p
pp
21
a tempo
strewn.
poch. rall.
a tempo
mp
mf
p
25
mp
mf
2. Then slow - ly I a - rose and left my loom, left my
pp
mp
p

29
mp
loom, And, in sor-row, wandered from my lone - ly room; A
mp
p
33
mf
my - riad stars were shin - ing, And all the heavens were bright and clear,
mp
mf
mp
p
p
mp
p
37
Bright with sil - v'ry ra-diance from the moon, from the moon, And the
mf
mp
41
mp
p rall.
a tempo
night - in - gale poured forth her sil - v'ry tune, sil - v'ry tune.
mp
p
pp
mp
p
pp

mp
3. Such
poch. rall.
a tempo
mp
p
pp
mf
beau-ty eased my heart, and I came home, I came home to my
p sempre tranquillo
mp
mp
p rall.
a tempo
loom, to my loom.
p
mp dolce
rall.
p
pp

6. ELFENLIED

ELFIN-SONG

(1888)

Eduard Mörike
(1804–75)
Translation by Jean Allister

HUGO WOLF
(1860–1903)

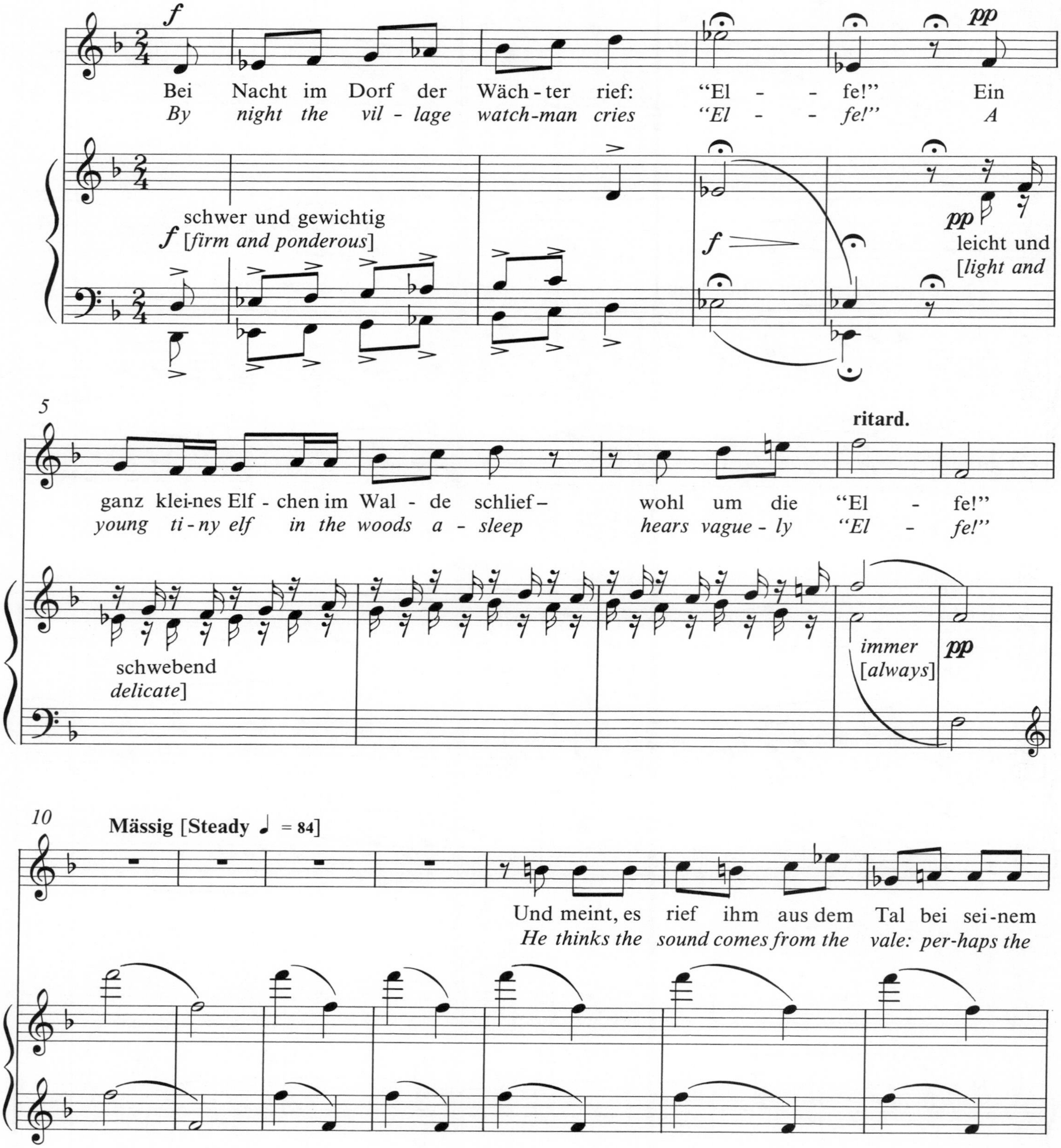

The original is a play on the word 'Elfe'. The watchman cries 'Elfe' (eleven o'clock); the sleepy little elf (Elfe) awakens, thinking he is being called.

17
poco rit.
a tempo
Na-men die Nach-ti - gall, o - der Sil - pe - lit hätt' ihm ge - ru - fen.
night - in-gale calls his name, or per - haps it is Sil - pe - lit call - ing.
22
Reibt sich der Elf' die Au - gen aus, be - gibt sich vor sein Schneck-en -
The lit - tle elf then rubs his eyes; he stands be - fore his ti - ny
ppp
26
- haus und ist als wie ein trun - ken Mann, sein Schläf-lein war nicht voll ge -
house and he is like a drunk - en man so sleep - y he can hard - ly
pp
30
- tan, und hum - pelt al - so, tip - pe, tapp, durchs Ha - sel - holz ins Tal hin -
stand. He hob - bles gent - ly on tip - toe through ha - zel wood to vale be -

34
-ab, schlupft an der Mau - er hin so dicht, da sitzt der Glüh-wurm Licht an
-low, creeps to the wall and crouch - es there where glow worms light the dark night
38
Licht.
air.
"Was
"What
pp
p
42
sind das hel - le Fen - ster - lein? Da drin wird ei - ne Hoch - zeit sein: die
are these win - dows shin - ing bright? It must be some - one's wed - ding night; the
ppp
46
Klei - nen sit - zen beim Mah - le, und trei - ben's in dem Saa - le.
lit - tle chil - dren are feast - ing, and ev - 'ry one shouts 'Greet - ing'.
ppp

bedeutend langsamer
[considerably slower]
50
Da guck' ich wohl ein we-nig 'nein!"
Per-haps a ti-ny peep I'll take."
schneller
[faster]
Pfui,
Oh,
mf
pp
zögernd
[hesitating]
entschlossen
[resolute]
sf
nicht eilen!
[don't hurry]
mässig
[steady]
sehr zart
[very tender]
53
p
stösst den Kopf an har-ten Stein! El-fe, gelt, du hast ge-nug? Gu-
bangs his head a-gainst the stone! Well now elf, is that e-nough? Cuck-
p
pp
57
-kuk! El - - fe, gelt, du hast ge-nug? Gu-
- oo! Well now elf, is that e-nough? Cuck-
61
[senza cresc.]
-kuk! Gu-kuk! Gu-kuk! Gu-kuk!
- oo! Cuck-oo! Cuck-oo! Cuck-oo!
senza cresc.
f

7. FAREWELL, YE LIMPID SPRINGS

from 'Jephtha' (1751)

Thomas Morell
(1703–84)

G. F. HANDEL
(1685–1759)

13
and years, and years of pain. Fare-well. Fare-well, fare-
16
-well, ye lim-pid springs, and floods, Fare-well, fare-well, thou bu-sy world, thou
19
bu-sy world, where reign Short hours of joy, and years of pain, and years
22
of pain, Short hours of joy, and years of pain. Fare-well,

Andante larghetto [♩ = 104]
25
[mf]
Fare-well, Fare-well! Bright - er scenes I seek a - bove,
[mf]
29
Bright - er scenes I seek a - bove,
33
[legato]
In the realms of peace and love, In the realms of
36
peace and love. Bright - er scenes I seek a-bove, In the realms of

40
peace and love, In the realms of peace and love.
44
Bright - er scenes I seek a - bove,
47
Bright-er scenes I seek a-bove, In the realms of peace and love.
51
Bright - er scenes I seek a-bove, Bright - er scenes I seek a - bove,
tr

55
[legato]
In — the realms of peace and love, — In the realms — of peace and love.
59
[crescendo]
Bright - er scenes I seek a - bove, In the realms of peace and — love.
Adagio
[f]
Tempo primo
[crescendo]
[f]
63
67
*suggested cadenza:
peace — and — love.
tr

8. DOMINE DEUS
from 'Gloria' RV589

Translation by Jean Allister

ANTONIO VIVALDI
(1678–1741)

16
Do - - - mi - ne De - us, Rex coe - le - stis, De - us Pa - ter,
Lord God Al-might-y, King of hea-ven, God the Fa - ther,
19
De - - us Pa - - - - - - - - - - - - ter, Pa-
God the Fa - - - - - - - - - - - - ther, our
22
- ter om - ni - po-tens.
Fa-ther, al-might-y Lord.
Do - - mi - ne
Lord God Al-
25
De - us, Do - - mi - ne De - us, Rex coe - le - stis,
- might-y, Lord God Al-might-y, King of hea - ven,
De - us Pa - ter, De - us
God the Fa - ther, God the

28
Pa - ter, Pa - - - - ter, Pa-
Fa - ther, Fa - - - - ther, our
31
-ter om-ni - po-tens, Pa - - -
Fa-ther al-might - y Lord, Fa - - -
34
- - - - - - - - ter, Pa-ter om-ni - po-tens.
- - - - - - - - ther, our Fa-ther al - might-y Lord.
VI-
37
40
-DE

9. EBBEN? NE ANDRÒ LONTANA
from 'La Wally' (1892)

Luigi Illica
(1857–1919)
*Translation by Jean Allister

ALFREDO CATALANI
(1854–93)

*This translation has been revised in bars 3–5 and 40–42 for this new edition.

13
-pian-to, è rim-pian-to, è do-lor!
soothe me, thus to soothe my grief and pain.
p
sonoro
18
[Più mosso ♩ = 72]
p dolciss. con espressione
O del-la ma-dre mia ca-sa gio-
Oh dear-est mo-ther, dear-est home so
pp
dolciss.
22
-con-da, la Wal-ly ne an-drà da te, da
hap-py, a-las, I must leave you now and
pp
25
animando
te lon-ta-na as-sa-i, e for-se a
ne-ver more re-turn here, and ne-ver

28
te, e for - se a te non fa -
more, and ne - ver more, ne - ver
31
f con anima
- rà mai più ri - tor - no, nè più la ri - ve - dra - -
more shall I re - turn here, re - turn to see you all once
f
34
[molto] ritard.
Tempo I
p
- i! mai più, mai più!
more, Fare - well, fare - well!
f
pp
37
pp
Ne an - drò so - la e lon -
And so, I must a -
ppp dolciss.

poco stent.
- ta - na co - me l'e - co del - la pia cam - pa - na,
- way now, church bells' e - cho fad-ing far be - hind me.
poco stent.
pp col canto
a tempo
cresc.
là, fra la ne - ve bian - ca; n'an - drò, n'an-
There to the snow - y mount - ains a - las, a -
- drò so - la e lon - ta - na
- las, a - lone I'll go then,
e fra le nu - bi d'ôr!
and ne-ver more re - turn.
dim.
pp

10. THE SNOW MAIDEN'S ARIA

from 'The Snow Maiden' (1881)

The original Russian text was by the composer, based on a play by Alexander Ostrovsky

N.A. RIMSKY-KORSAKOV
(1844–1908)

17
poco rit.
Sing - ing roun - de - lays and danc - ing all the while, Songs of joy to fête the
20
a tempo
a piacere allargando
com - ing of the spring, "Hi, La - - - do, my
p
24
a tempo
poco animato
Lell!"
That is my
pp
mf dimin.
29
dream, and my de - light, I live for me - lo - dy a - lone.
p
f

34 Recit.
mf
Oh let me go, and when you shall re – turn in win – ter – time,
sfpp
40
Adagio [♩ = 52]
in dim and som-bre woods, at fall of eve I'll sing for you
pp
46
Charm – ing your sol – i – tude and while the time a – way, hap – py songs I
52
poco rit.
poco più animato
stringendo
learned with joy. Lell shall teach me all I know,
pp

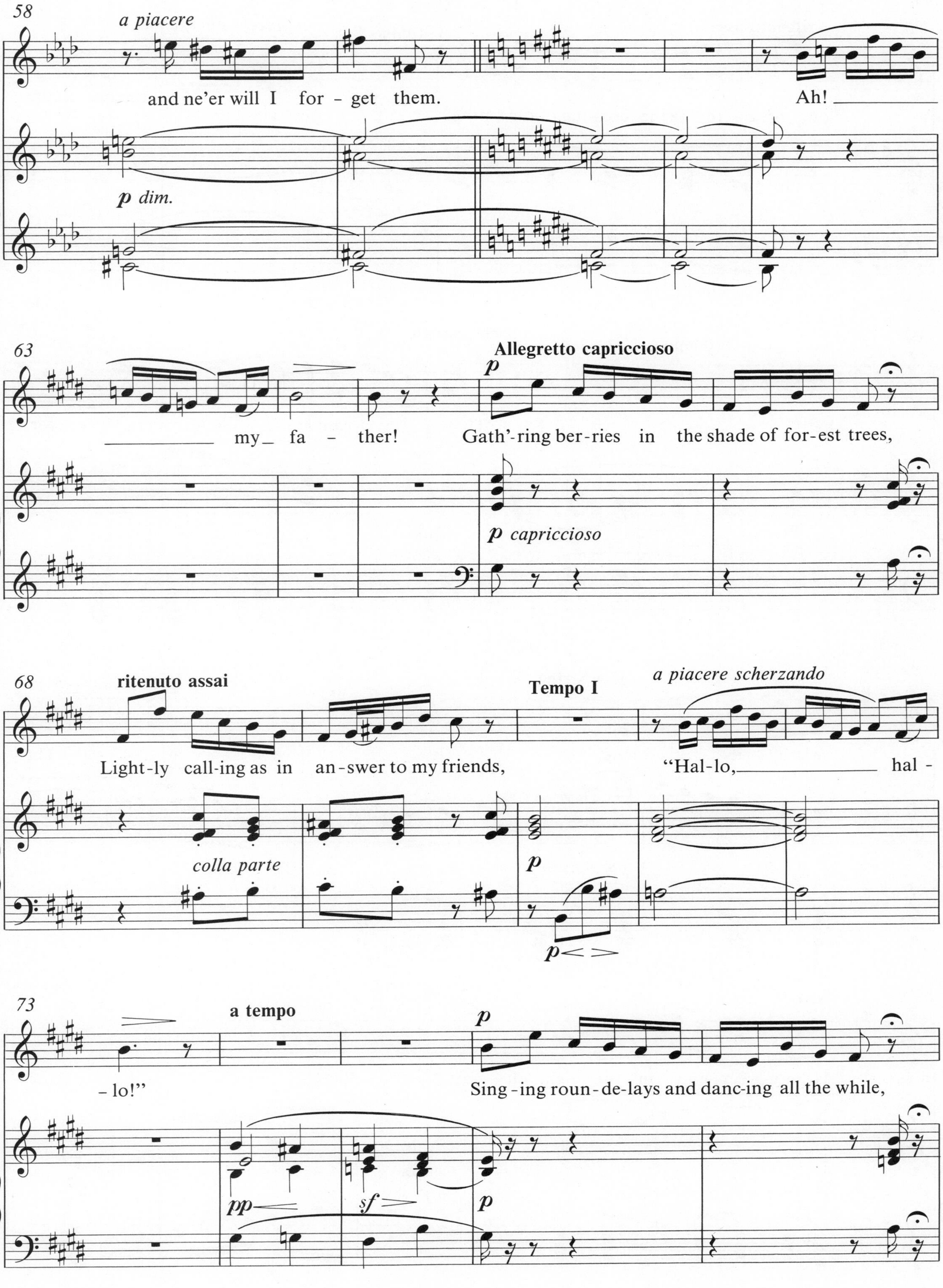
58
a piacere
and ne'er will I for - get them.
Ah!
p dim.
63
Allegretto capriccioso
p
my_ fa - ther! Gath'-ring ber-ries in the shade of for-est trees,
p capriccioso
68
ritenuto assai
Tempo I
a piacere scherzando
Light-ly call-ing as in an-swer to my friends, "Hal-lo, hal -
colla parte
p
73
a tempo
p
- lo!" Sing-ing roun-de-lays and danc-ing all the while,
pp
sf
p

Processed and printed by
Halstan & Co. Ltd., Amersham, Bucks., England